PRAISE FOR

Dirt Songs

"Those last afternoons we walked the tracks hand in hand,/ making up songs, going nowhere." These final lines of "Photo 1985" are two of many that will haunt me long after reading Kari Gunter-Seymour's new book, a collection alive with lust, music, lost boys, lost dogs, food pantries, divorce, deployment, booze, birds, and love for a land buzzing with abundance. I admire the swagger and wisdom of this voice and the raw tenderness with which the poet greets her subjects, here and gone, present and past. A celebration and a dirge, *Dirt Songs* is a moving tribute to a place and its people.

—KATHY FAGAN, author of *Bad Hobby*

The poems in this exuberant and loving book arise from a time in late-20th century America that was not so loving, dissolved and diluted, as some of us who lived in smaller places began to feel isolated and abandoned by bigger culture and a bigger economy. It was a deeply confusing time. Those of us who lived in smaller and less enlightened communities were lured to believe there was something bigger and brighter we should belong to, and the actual communities in which we lived were somehow lacking. Other forces were at work as well, and only now, after many years of collapse, can we realize the ruse to which out of the way places were subjected. And yet, the spirit and wisdom of the local sense of belonging remains. The stark and often darkly funny poems in this collection suggest a re-direction is in order. It's a sense of return, and I find the poems here offer a loving and hopeful suggestion that such a return is possible. This is a book of many things, small and large, but it always tells its reader that poetry in its most honest rendering, is always a way forward. This is a book to celebrate and be glad we have it with us.

—MAURICE MANNING, author of *Railsplitter*

I read these poems to hear home—where we "warsh" our hands before "fixin to go"—these poems crafted with the art of saying the way that we say. This collection is a musical archive of a place, which could be Meigs County or the foothills, Huntington or Harlan. A place called Appalachia, where 'it isn't ever delicate to live." A place oft missing from the American imagination, where lives "fold into themselves like letters/ in envelopes . . . squirreled away." Kari deeply honors the reality of this place, this people. She is a poet who serves. These poems made me cry as they sang to me, like a grandparent singing hymns from another room. Bring your "sack of sorrows/ laid open—perch on soil" with this storyteller, and find in these *Dirt Songs*, "a litany to hold off morning."

—Joy Priest, author of *Horsepower*

Kari Gunter-Seymour has spun an absolute marvel in her new poetry collection *Dirt Songs*. Each of these poems leads you down a path, leading you, by the last verse, to a surprisingly deeper place, with each section of the collection opening a richer, broader trajectory. *Dirt Songs* opens in the Appalachia of the late seventies, a place where, as Gunter-Seymour writes, "marijuana grew thick behind barns,/ alongside butterfly weed and gray-headed coneflowers" but the speaker of these poems travels through, pulling the tripwires in our minds, until we get to a present-day Appalachia where, as Gunter-Seymour writes, "you probably don't know tax dollars paid/ fifty bucks a head to kill sixty-eight thousand/ coyotes in 2019, or that forty-six percent/ of Appalachian school-aged children/ were food insecure the same year." The poems in this collection are linked throughout by this dazzle, of a personal history that entwines with the cultural and political, and readers will come away from this collection with an understanding of the way the speaker has inserted herself—and others—into the quoin of history: to follow each of these poems is to land solidly on the best unease existent. These poems both delight and displace. To hear one of Gunter-Seymour's dirt songs is to listen, intently, to the symphony of the human condition.

—Jacinda Townsend, author of *Saint Monkey* and *Mother Country*

Dirt Songs

poems

Kari Gunter-Seymour

EASTOVER
— PRESS —

Dirt Songs

Kari Gunter-Seymour

POETRY
ISBN   978-1-958094-35-8

Book & Cover Design ~ EK LARKEN

Cover Image ~ Rachel Claire [PEXELS]

———————

EastOver Press encourages the use of our publications in educational settings. For questions about educational discounts, contact us online: www.EastOverPress.com or info@EastOverPress.com.

PUBLISHED IN THE UNITED STATES OF AMERICA BY

EASTOVER
— PRESS —

ROCHESTER, MASSACHUSETTS
www.EastOverPress.com

Dirt Songs

Also by Kari Gunter-Seymour

Alone in the House of My Heart
A Place So Deep Inside America It Can't Be Seen
Serving (chapbook)

CONTENTS

One

Two

Three

To all the invisible girls

One

We wash into this world, a pair of raised eyebrows, delivered from one floating world to another.

Eye of Newt, Toe of Frog

Where I'm from, girls learn
to conjure young—a dash of salt flung,
I lick my pointer finger, spin
three times, call forth the tufted trills
of wild beak and bone flute.

Early on, I partnered up, roused
with hope. What I got was someone
else's stiff neck, the shape
of someone else's arrogance
siphoning the pith from my spine.

My hollow bird bones winnow
stories I don't want to hear,
I shush each saga—too much
prattle, unweighted,
could damn well loose a demon.

Because My Ancestors

I taught myself who I was
by sounding out my name,
heard the word for wanting
commingling my veins, a salty pulse,
letters disguised as life.

I was the silk gown my mother
would never own, the black dust
of coal-fraught mountains, the face
of my grandmothers and all who came
before, staring back from tintypes,
the copper taste of feminine rust.

My restless breaths shouldered
their way, history's finger to its lips,
impatient with my niggling.
I quarried roots, digging in
like my great-grandfather's oxen
dragging a crusty plow,

a need in my belly, sagas flashing
against my back, the stories—
my people, crossing a cratered land,
a pregnant woman, lanky and twanged,
a thick muscled man, farsighted,
timbered the land, planted seeds,
prayed for rain, the soil so rich,
so ripe with possibility.

Me Oh, My Oh

The pond below the house reflects
heaven no matter the weather.
A pair of Canada geese park themselves
along the edge, honk disapprovals
as me and Sadie Jae fly by

in her Jeep four-by-four, singing
Jambalaya, crawfish pie and a fillet gumbo.
Wind wicks our ponytails, prickles
our sun-burned shoulders, pilfers

our whiskey breath. We spin ruts into
the lower pasture, dart in, out of the pines,
come to a slide-into-home-plate stop, inches
from the front stoop, our laughter lawless.

Times when I go low,
I summon that sizzley summer,
ear to the wind, listen
for Sadie's spicy Cajun yodels.

Bad Company

Electric bass guitar riffs, magnified
times ten, subwoofers mounted to metal signposts,
Paul Rodgers' moany lyrics thrust every direction,
his voice alone enough to slick the thighs
of every female high schooler, standing
sweat soaked, in line—senior trip,
Kings Island 1979, headbanging, hips wanging
side-to-side, arms thrown wide, waiting
to ride The Beast—tallest, fastest, longest wood
roller coaster in the world, the boys spurting
predictable agonies and pheromones.
Wasn't long before Emmy Bond and Jeff Bevans
were all over each other, tongues tangling.
I pretended not to see him slip a hand inside
her shorts, ignored the way her head flew back.
I won't say whether I let one of those rowdy boys
do the five-finger shop and cop underneath
my tank top during the long bus ride home.
But it was frigging hot that day, I'll give you that.

Amesville Girls

sip Squirt soda from lime green
returnable glass bottles pulled ice cold from
the chest cooler at Kasler's corner grocery,
retrieve the dime, stuff it in the jukebox
at Fanny's Family Diner, dance

the Bus Stop or the Sprinkler
to AC/DC, say words like *warsh*
and *fixin' to go*, spit watermelon seeds
good as the boys, swim naked in the crick,

sneak out to sleep in the graveyard
to be closer to their grannies,
ink ballpoint tattoos on each other's biceps,
wear fruity red lip gloss to softball practice,

dream Guns N' Roses' tour bus
stops for lunch at the diner
and Slash or Duff McKagan
kiss their cherry mouths, finger
their buttons, white-knight them away.

Where We Come from Can Break Us

She was curious, always questions
from that one, a nine-year-old
going on twenty, sneaking
the backwoods to my porch swing,
earless to her mama's played-out rebukes.

I was a new mother, alone
more than was fit.
The baby loved her singing
and she would brush my hair
for hours, jawing tales
about her made up life.

I often think of her hangdog
eyes and heavy lashes,
hope she was able to save herself
from that broke down place.
Who'm I trying to kid?

Hit Me Baby One More Time

Thirty years out
my high school bestie sends
a friend request.
I figure what the hell.

Back in the day we were inseparable,
wore each other's clothes,
hot-boxed cigarettes up in her attic
bedroom, windows open
no matter the weather, pushed
spent butts through an odd cranny
in a vase shaped like a man's head,
watched tufts of smoke chimney out.

We'd dance to FM radio, gossip,
concoct stories, lie side by side on her hard,
rugless floor, pinkies locked,
listen to her mom and dad downstairs,
soused on whiskey, throwing
heartless words and whatever breakables
were handy at each other.

She DMs me:
I miss the friendship we had.
I am sober 3½ years now,
have a lot of people to atone to.

I don't want to be atoned.
I buried that shit long ago,
sure as Sherlock not
going to dredge it up now.
All thumbs and shaky fingers,
I click *Unfriend.*

That Plus Fifty Cents

We christened it The Sharpsburg Mall—Sharpsburg, a township of three houses, a Methodist church, and The Mall. The owner, miser, creeper of the highest order, we dubbed Buzzard, after his peculiar nose and the way he constantly circled his domain, stink-eyed customers, squawking *you break it, you bought it*. We would get stoned, crack open a few beers, set out to The Mall for a laugh. On the counter near the cash register sat stacks of colored condoms, motor oil, used comic books, rolling papers, *Hustler Magazine*. There were racks of chips, cupboards of cellophaned clumps, a dilapidated cooler filled with ice and questionable swill. Sheltered in shadow in the far-right corner, an ancient vending machine leaned, cock-eyed, glass scratched, a series of pull knobs along the bottom, crudely drawn question marks scotch taped above each knurl. Two quarters and a firm tug would bang out a plastic easter egg, inside the egg a fortune, typed up tidy by Buzzard himself, who turned out to have a knack for divination by way of cheeky haiku. We laughed our asses off week after week, until the night Jaycee Lynn wrecked her pickup during a downpour, crumpled fortune in her left hand:

> sad clouds overhead
> cold raindrops stinging and black
> wings of daylight dead

Our Grandmother

twisted silver-streaked strands
into a knot, pinned at the tip of her crown,
draped her bird bones in crossback aprons
cut from calico, sewn on a pump pedal Singer,
bought brand new just after the war,

baked flakey scratch biscuits
from White Lily flour, spoonfuls
of lard, a pinch of salt and sass,
danced the flatfoot clog around
an old wringer washer,
employed on Mondays without fail,

wielded a scythe and hoe
good as any man, grew cabbages
big as watermelons,
drew us maps, where we came from,
patchworks of bloodroot, furled fierce
along the face of the Appalachians,

orphaned us, laid out
under a pine branch blanket,
a rough-chiseled stone.
Redbuds wept purple pearls,
the fields so bare they grew voices.

Mysterious Ways

Nine weeks, no monthlies,
my body a nestling's perch,
a tremoring tree, leaning

into a southeaster, hard luck
and poverty licking red-hot
flames against my bent back.

I scrimped, saved, still forty dollars
short of the cash I'd need to set
me and that little bird free.

No stranger to a bowed head,
I got straight to the appeal, laid out
my endgame and trading points.

The Lord coughed up two twenties
by way of a birthday card, sent postage due
from my Granny, who wrote at length

about her late-night vision. She saw
me old, alone in the dark,
crying out for some little bird.

Oreo

Sugar words, all cocoa
and bonbon

your vanilla mouth
wrapped round

them coos you use
all creamy—your tongue

swirling the stuff
sandwiched between

my legs, for a spell
forget

why
they were made

How Could a Woman

He could not climb in the driver's
seat without lighting up a joint.
There I'd be, juggling bunting, bottle,
binky, strapping the baby in his car seat,
while my husband sat, rolling a fat one,
lip-syncing whatever was blasting
from the radio, sealing the deal
with nimble finger work,
a slick slip of the tongue.
He would key the ignition, flip open
a lighter, take a long slow toke,
cough hard enough to crack a rib,
ease into gear. What soured me most
was how pleased he was with himself,
that and the fact I stuck with him
for close on two years.

Hanky-Panky Poker

We women dressed as if headed
to the French Riviera—frilly skirts,
teased-up hairdos, shiny lip gloss.
The men wore flannel shirts,
stunk of sour mash and tobacco.

It got intense. Five Card Draw,
nickel ante, quarter limit—
Texas Hold'em if we drank tequila shots.
There were some shining moments
before the whole shebang went briny.

Sarah Sipple called a nature break,
gone too long to the facilities
and Sonny Munford who'd stepped outside
to do the same, got caught bare-assed,
Levi's around his ankles, rutting Sarah
like some randied white tail buck.

All things considered, we switched
to Euchre, less hard liquor,
more chips and dip.
Sonny Munford went tail-ass-tits to the wind.
Phil Sipple got hisself a new partner.

Bada Bing Bada Boom

He was so damn good—
had a look, cocky smile, a lock of hair
loose across his forehead, dark eyes
that could melt a cold steel rail.

He'd saunter up, smelling of heat
and lightning, move in, lips to my ear,
one finger, trailing my cheekbone
and downward, firing me up.
A living room chair, our kitchen table,
various lamps and half-filled
mason jars, fell prey to our fervor.

Until they didn't. Until his unkempt
hair and juvenile gyrating grew tiresome,
his pranks predictable.
There were mouths to feed, bills to pay,
his excuses an endless replay
of teenage tantrums and there I was,
working my ass off for chump change,
a bag full of if onlys.

Mostly a Cage Is Air

His fingers, cold as metal,
locked across her mouth,
clumps of her feathers
wrenched from their sockets,
she tucks herself, like a folded note
into a shadowed roost between
the stairs and her small iron gate,
dreams a billow of sky, wings,
perpetual winds.

Spring in the Hollow

Beryl blue sky,
sun in our eyes,

creek nuzzles stone.
Breeze stirs, reminds us

this ground we tramp,
root labyrinth,

rising and setting inside our shoes,
is remedy—electric

with violets, dandelion and fern,
a single buzzing bee.

Any flaw our bodies carry
from *otherwhere*

disappears—
at waterfall,

at ravine edge,
inside the unstoppable petal storm.

Carolina Kin

Tether-born—thorns on a rosebush,
heritors of the hive, chroniclers
of who done what to who.
Nostalgia mongers, lined up like leftovers
wrapped in Tupperware or tin foil,
children clutched to calico aprons,
shy as bat-eared foxes,
moony as moths hitting a windshield.

Counterparts—cocksure, lanky,
all ribs and sternums, head cupped palms,
ball caps tucked low, oily rags in back pockets,
twang-hinged lips spitting tobacco
and local politics astride a string of hexes,
language clear as morning fog.

Inside the house—tintypes trim the mantle,
holdovers trussed up, Sundayfied,
clinging to Bibles and boggy timbers,
opaque around the edges—his eyes, her nose,
ancestral gap between front incisors.

Back of the barn—pats on the back,
slap of a knee, fiddle, banjo,
tang of Bar-B-Que, cob corn and 'taters,
spice of the loblolly pines.

Salt of the Earth

Handsome, too, one of five brothers,
tiny mama who wasn't above
slapping the piss out of a fella.

He loved him some blow—his only vice.
When he and Sadie Jae hooked up,
we reckoned she'd put the kybosh
to all of that and she did,

until the night Pete Slater brought
a speedball to Saturday night Euchre.
Everybody knows Belushi, Joplin, Hendrix.
This poem here is for Presley Potter—
give you the shirt off his back.

Sometimes I Picture You Walking Too Far Ahead

We wore Carhartt bibs, Red Wing boots,
denim ball caps turned backwards,
smoked Marlboros, ganja when we could get it,
drank Everclear and Hawaiian Punch
mixed in Ronald McDonald collector cups,

sang Cyndi Lauper's *Time After Time*,
Bonnie Raitt's *Something to Talk About*,
rode the ridges on a used Yamaha 1100.
Local boys called us dykes
because we wouldn't put out.

But I quit the quaaludes right after
we woke up soaking wet under a beech tree
outside a town neither of us recognized.

You'd get fired up, unbuckle your bibs,
skinny dip anytime there was a full moon,
claiming your ginormous breasties
would keep you afloat indefinitely,

spout on about whose ass you'd like to kick,
the latest fool who tried to kiss you,
your up-to-the-minute political twaddle,
sung loud and purposefully off pitch.

To this day, neighbors go out of their way
to describe drowning as a peaceful passing.
All I know is this loneness of body,
curse the way my legs still carry me forward.

True Grit

Sweet Child O'Mine
spun throaty on the boombox,
only CD I owned. The baby
squatted in his second-hand
Jolly Jumper, clipped at the top
of the door frame—bouncing
as if the floor was a trampoline,
he an Olympic trainee.

I took the afternoon off work
to have my wisdom teeth pulled,
groggy from the laughing gas,
ticked off at my spouse,
who'd obviously been rolling joints,
leaving behind a whole mess
of seeds and stems, brushed
from coffee table to shoddy carpet.

Behind on the electric bill,
car tires bald, the twit once
hocked my high school class ring
to buy an ounce of pot.

I admit it. I allowed myself
to be diminished way too long.
I might never have culled my courage
had it not been for the baby,
the way he carefully cupped my jaw
as I lifted him from the jumper.
Love is or it ain't.

Granny Medicine

Perceptive, picky, Granny forages
along fencerow and thicket,
her quilted pouch slung crossways,
arms tucked tight to ribs,
thwarting a bramble's lash.

Crows attend her, gusting
their long voweled language.
Spring winds poke wild fingers
through the trees, a weeping cherry
casts pink petals along her path.

Beneath damp pines she plucks
needles and licorice root to soothe
a scratchy throat, stiff knuckles loosen
white oak bark for fever, a pinch
of wormwood to calm the nerves.

Along the creek's muddy skin,
yellow root and comfrey she'll mash
into salve, wild violets and red clay
for poultices, mullein and pink clover,
honey infused, to coat a cough.

Bundling sage into a burly stick,
she smudges the cabin, burns
mugwort shavings to call the spirits,
packs a ginseng chew between cheek
and gum to fight fatigue—waits.

Outside her window, crows cluster,
their shadows long, heads
bent low, as if in prayer,
as if they know, more than once,
she has stolen a body back from death.

Child of the Large-Beaked Bird

The crows are up to no good,
tapping the tin roof like it's
Miss Glover's School for Awkward Girls,
all juke, jig and ja-ja.
My granddog doesn't approve,
not the rooftop trapeze or the tomfoolery
in the garden, mischievous pecks
gouged around the scarecrow's eyes.

They're toying with me.
I've tried to bribe them—
fresh fruit, cat food, sequins,
propped myself nearby,
full lotus, trilling.

Why subject myself and this prized
pooch to the insufferable?
The Indigenous say their ancestors
came to earth in the form of Crow.
I come to them, my sack of sorrows
laid open—perch on soil
my ancestors stole, sing dirt songs.

Two

Some stories fold into themselves like letters into envelopes, tied with ribbon, squirreled away.

Photo 1985

There you are, cherub-faced, rice cake with peanut butter,
and little Willie Thompson, balancing yourselves up against
that old house in need of paint, your hair curling up
in the noonday heat. I remember those Oshkosh bibs and tiny
red tennis shoes, and how not long after, we made plans
to leave the farm without your father. That summer I grew

pole beans and Roma tomatoes in raised beds
filled with bottom land soil and cow manure
pushed up the hillsides in a tottering wheelbarrow.
By fall, multicolored jars lined the cellar shelves while
zip-locked zucchini loaves rested in the deep freeze,
awaiting snowy days when we'd huddle together, grateful

for our hand-me-down wood burner. I miss the smell
of lilac from the heirloom bush where you would hide
and the cooing pair of mourning doves perched on those
electric wires just outside the kitchen window, ever marking
the day we left Meigs County, where marijuana grew thick
behind barns, alongside butterfly weed and gray-headed coneflowers.
Those last afternoons we walked the tracks hand in hand,
making up songs, going nowhere.

After the Farm, the Apartment on Hope Drive

Just the two of us, cramped city dwellers,
subsidized and lonely, listening
to the McKinley boys thumping their Big Wheel
across our ceiling, their daddy shouting
one of you boys better fetch me another beer.
Giving me shivers recalling the streaks of red and purple
mushroomed crosswise on their mama's face,
always thankful when it grew quiet,
even knowing all the lights were out
and neither of those boys had scrubbed their teeth.

Beside myself, finding you
and Timmy Moreland crouched behind
that Ninja Turtles sandbox cover,
dodging BBs from his brother's Red Rider
which got taken away only after he shot
clean through their Magnavox,
causing his maw-maw to miss her favorite
America's Funniest Home Videos.

That Christmas you played with G.I. Joes
bought from the dollar store, delivered by Santa.
We baked sugar cookies from scratch,
rode the bus downtown to see the lights.
Many a sleepless night, long after
tucking you in, I flipped on the swag light
hanging over the kitchen table, sat down
to notebook and pen, waiting for the next words
to come. Turns out the danger in the writing,
is you will remember all you've worked so hard to erase.

Fool's Spring

One of those deceitful February days
in southeastern Ohio
that splits open, pretends it's spring,
the air dances.

I was on my own, my son
with his thick-brained dad,
court ordered. I blame nostalgia,
the instigator that sent me eastward,

back to my hometown,
to Travis and Ivy,
Saturday afternoons, whisky neat,
Euchre, cheating spouses.

I told myself, I needed the land,
gravel roads, muddy creek bottoms,
but I knew if anyone was holding
it'd be them—smudged mirror,

ace of spades scraping lean white lines,
a rolled up twenty-dollar bill.
It had been years since
I'd tried to ruin my life.

That morning, I let lose
my hair, cranked Willie & Waylon
on the car's stereo, pretended
I was pure cont'ry again.

State Route 32 Appalachian Highway

If you get lucky one steamy afternoon,
held hostage by summer's
endless orange barrels, you'll spot
the tall blonde roadman.
Tan, sweat glazing his body
like pricey massage oil, tight jeans,
burly biceps, bushy mustache.
Imagine him after work,
a dark bar—*Bikers Way Lounge*
or *Smiling Skull Saloon,*
ice cold Pabst Blue Ribbon,
God Bless the USA on the jukebox.

A "knowing" will wash over you.
Behind those sunglassed eyes,
green maybe blue, is a promise:
Girl, I could do things...

Lord have mercy, the musk
of newly laid blacktop,
testosterone and humidity,
is enough to make a girl swoonish.

If the Fates are truly generous,
the skinny flagger boy wrangling traffic
will pause, confused, his walkie-talkie
pushed tight against his cheek.
Sweet Jesus, yes, boy, make this endless
line of vehicles linger.
Let you see that studly man's curly
mane shake loose from hard hat,
forearm across slick brow,
thick fingers firm on his handle,
thrusting, forward and back,
forward and back, his machine

inching slowly, skillfully,
his apparatus nearly parallel
with your SUV, its ejaculations
spurting and powerful.

You may need to loosen a button,
adjust your skirt, spread sticky thighs,
as any woman would in that kind of heat,
finger-fluff the back of your hair.
Curse unrestrained as you whack
your knee, hard against the steering wheel,
courtesy of the drivers behind,
honk-honking and who can blame them?
Flagger-boy, damn it to hell,
has set loose the horde.

Bet You Think You're Special

It came on me like the darkening
of day. He was handsome,
it was late, his lopsided grin,
the band, the booze, his Chevy King Cab,
air-conditioned, backseat leathered
and wide, his fingers thick,
tongue a freaking bang-fanger.

He knew exactly when to shut up.

We staggered back inside,
the smell of fireworks
and detonations all up inside us.
She stood there, wraith-like,
woeful but tearless,
infant on one hip, toddler
fist-clinched to the other.
Some smiles are all teeth.

The Thing About Your Dad

I could lay on the guilt,
say, if you keep avoiding your dad
you'll end up like him.
Bitch your own Karma.
Not like if you got caught
with a joint or skanked
on someone's girlfriend.
I'm talking about *divine decree*.

I would be the first to admit
his heartless disregard is the worst.
Not even a postcard
the whole time you were in Iraq.
Though there was that one summer
he taught you all the words
to *Rubber Soul* and to shave
even before you needed to.

Off the tracks more than a little,
he said it made him mental,
thinking of ways other people
could fuck up perfectly good lives.

You're wasting years, Son.
Simple math.
A person can't go around
telling people what to do
with their lives long as he has,
without eventually believing
he knows what he's talking about.

Serving

Remember that time your dog died and I didn't tell you for months
because you had deployed and George Bush was shouting,
Bring it on and we were all thinking Korea was fixing to blow.
But when I emailed to say we were headed for West Virginia,
you fired back, *Mom, where is Annie?* and I had to say she was hit by a car.
I sent brownies loaded with black walnuts from the old homeplace.

Or when you called me from Iraq asking me to talk to people
about donating shoes and I told you it was hopeless
because of the tsunami, everyone was already donating.
You said *Hell with that,* and your unit threw in their paychecks,
bought all those families just outside Fallujah new shoes off the Internet.
I made two hundred popcorn balls wrapped in wax paper.

Or that February you came home for R&R, so sad and sick.
I baked your favorite, meatloaf, and you said you couldn't possibly,
but I gave you doe-eyes, so you ate and threw up all night,
into the next day, saying over and over *Sweet Jesus, please,
make it stop* and I knew you weren't talking about the meatloaf.

Or the day after Sergeant Bentley went to Vegas and blew
his head off in the hotel bathroom, while here at home your best friend
got arrested for selling narcotics and you said neither one of them
needed to and maybe wouldn't have if you'd been there. So, I shipped
molasses cookies thick with Crisco frosting, all the way to Kandahar.

Or the afternoon your farm boy fingers tried to clamp the artery
on that baby girl, near the valley of Arghandab,
while her father screamed for Allah and blood soaked your uniform
when you hugged her to you as she passed.
I drenched that fruitcake in brandy for three days.

But mostly it was the night your daughter was born and we
locked eyes across the birthing room. I thought to myself,
skillet-fried chicken with candied sweet potatoes, fried okra,
lima beans with bacon, cornbread and Aunt Margaret's hot fudge cake.
We used the good dishes and Grandpa Oris said the blessing.

No Word from Kandahar

You begged to go fishing,
cut a hole in the ice.
Please, Mama.
I'll bait the hooks myself.

Come spring
you asked again.
Wrapped a picnic
in an old bandanna.

Trial and error,
life jacket strapped,
you found harbor
in the stillness where
both boy and fish seek prize.

Lord help me.
I would gladly bleed
to have you here tonight
on that rough rock bench,
cane pole in hand,
each breath a puff of frost.

Legitimate Cockamamie

If I mow the grass today,
it will just need mowing
again next week, which
reminds me, I need
to shave my legs,
though in my defense,
I do believe
I have earned the right
to let my leg hairs grow long.
I should run more,
which reminds me
of my menopause belly,
my body shaming,
the anger and sadness
of my adolescence.
How I let other people
dress me in their dreams,
learned to flaunt scabs
and scars like badges.
Which reminds me
of my grandmother,
her apple breath urging,
live, baby girl, live!
It's not wrong to want,
stand strong in my power,
make mental sculptures
of promises, spray paint
them with graffiti,
drag a camp chair
from the porch,
kick back beneath
the silver maple,
listen for the cold clicks
of creek water,
keep my heart-fire lit
so love can find me.

Golden Hour

Her perch a ladderback rocker
creaking the front porch,
she barely manages

to breathe in morning's scent,
latch on to the colors,
before mountain air
skyjacks that clutch of memories.

Others scurry
beneath weathered floorboards,
keep the dead company.
Oak shadows kneel
to know the dirt.

I watch her palsied hands
make a gesture, as if
letting go a bird.

Dew drops glitter the grass,
the light of her
the nearest I know to holy.

It Isn't Ever Delicate to Live

She felt like last night's wine bottle,
nothing left inside but grainy, bitter bits.
In a magazine at the veterinarian's office,
she read women over fifty obsess
about mortality. These days, she thinks
less about death, than of living too long,
impoverished, her life a footnote
in the Baptist church bulletin.
A woman who rarely cried though
she might be better for it, awake night
after night, imagining a life, brittle bones
jutting her calico fleece. No wonder
she was talking to the air, walking
the deer track home alone, jaw clinched,
a worn leash and empty collar
clutched dearly to her chest.

I Can Explain

Here in the foothills, every story begins
because somebody opens her mouth.
My great aunt turned ninety this month.
She can still recite all the names,
82 dead, Poston Mine Number 6, Millfield.
My cousin weeps first-hand experience
regarding Freedom Industries'
gross negligence along the Elk River.

It is no revelation that a lot of you
blame us for our twang and Billy Ray Cyrus,
for coal's carbon footprint
and *Make America Great Again.*

There's a kid with a mullet who lives
near me whose pickup truck wields
a giant Trump flag, so large
he almost ran off the road,
the flap obstructing his windshield.
I saw him erecting it in the Piggly Wiggly
parking lot like he was doing the most
patriotic thing ever.

Listen, he's a good kid—volunteers
at the dog shelter, first one out
to shovel on snow days.
So much of this willfulness is dependent
on generations having been born here,
knowing for a fact that poverty
is not a moral failing or the result
of not working hard enough.

His great, great, great grandfather
died at Poston Mine Number 6,
having volunteered an extra shift;

his granddad, in Vietnam.
His father works two jobs and serves
as Deacon at the First Baptist Church.

I don't know about you, but far beyond
the sermon, it's the music that pulls me in.
Those gospel sagas steeped in survival
and hallelujah, God's hands all over you.
I'll fly away, Oh glory, I'll fly away!

To touch another with what has touched
ourselves—isn't that the reason
humans developed language,
to build community, words drawn
from gesture and song, tales shared
in caves or on some lonesome prairie
under a gleaming night sky—overtures
brimming with light and air.

I can't help but think a lot of you
have never learned to relish your breath
or paused considerably to contemplate stars.
Do unto others, we say—
but you don't want to hear that story.

Land Lessons

She's lived here all her life,
a gift to know this land, its seasons,
tastes, smells, mindful of its wants—
even knowing every acre was once taken
by violence. We all have mortifications,
history's footprints threaded among the trees.

From the porch, sunset paints the surface
of the pond, pregnant with twigs
and twitchy insects, a Gaia of breeze
strums shuffled reeds.
She's had a good cry, one that could
have left a lesser woman sharp-cornered.

Later she will wash the dishes,
her face splashed and wakened,
her life unremarkable as the house fly
balanced on her dinner plate,
rubbing its bristly bowed legs together.

Family Curse

A kid, unwitting witness,
I watch my dad weep,
throw up in the utility room sink,
my mother's face caught
between what I now know
was confusion and repugnance.
In 1967 dads were not supposed
to cry or mothers shout,
Christ's sake, throw out the pills.
Why should he?
Doctors prescribed valium
like it was a multivitamin.

I saw my sister today.
We are estranged.
Life's a shitshow, she sighs,
pitiable eyes, bone thin,
but I finagled a scrip from the clinic.
Valium. A bump at breakfast,
another in the afternoon.
She asks, genuine in affection,
if I want any.

When Nature Takes Back One of Her Own

Years we curled beneath
that maple, backs against bark—
an embroidery of shadows,
a carpet of moss to cradle our bones.

Late summer's dog days
ushered ruthless storms,
every deluge a tug, even the grass
came unpinned—a reminder,
nothing is fixed or impervious,
peace a notion that ebbs and swells.

Leaves withered, fell, crusty tears,
sallow valentines—too many.
We wheelbarrowed soil, spoon-fed
fertilizers, strapped nylon cords
from trunk to tent stakes,
whispered incantations,

watched its grievous surrender,
branches flailing, a woosh, a thud,
a crackled exhalation, laying itself down
in starless dusk—leaving us,
every night bird, beetle and cricket
gulping for air.

The Dogwoods at Night

You got to see this, my husband spouts,
fresh in from tilling the fields,
scented in soil and diesel fuel from the tractor,
face lit up like a toddler straddling a pony.

It's dark, I'm in my pajamas,
freshly scrubbed, feet bare.
Grab your shoes, he says,
barn-bound to fire up the ATV.

Trainers laced, wrapped in a jacket,
I climb in beside him, the Teryx
idling full tilt, like it, too, can hardly
wait to see the spectacle that has
my earthbound man star-eyed.
Off we ride to the lower pasture,
headlights blazing.

When we get there, he doesn't
say a word, doesn't need to.
The high beams refract off clusters
of pearly petals, chandeliers, neon-lit,
psychedelic. Branches arched,
we cruise beneath cathedral ceilings
in low gear, mouths flung open,
gasping up wonder by the lung full.

When we finally return to the house,
shimmery-glazed and chilly,
he hugs me so tight, I smell
the sweat, the oily rags, the hammer,
nails, screwdrivers of him, my heart
pounding out symphonies and sonnets.

Pawpaws Are Ripe

Bumper crop, enough to sate tastebuds,
skins split open on the spot, pulp scooped
fingers-to-mouth, the rest collected
for sweet breads, hand-churned ice cream,

home brewed beer. I smile at all the ways
my people have come to preserve
this delicate fruit, one of the few treasures
of this ridge not yet stripped or clear cut,

fragrant like a ripe banana, hints
of strawberry, pineapple, mango,
flesh creamy yellow, spicy
brown seeds—same sown centuries ago

by Shawnee, Delaware and Mingo.
Once a year I harvest, render, reflect,
return seeds to native soil, on my knees,
every turn of the trowel a benediction.

Sweet Corn and Watermelon

Because he had no shoes of any count
he had to be clever about his steps.
The trail led through the woods,
no school buses in those days.
Boys carried twenty-twos
in case rabid skunks or wild dogs
or something edible showed itself.

A boy can learn a lot about life
in bare feet, once the weather turns,
rags tied to his feet.
Snowbound, he can lose some toes
trying to bring in firewood,
his belly empty for days unless
his daddy has luck tracking
or the preacher makes it through
with offerings from the Baptists.
Lord knows if his mama had been alive
things might have been different.

These fields, now wedged in pre-fab
and cul-de-sac, your great-great plowed
and seeded by mule, scythe and hoe.
I want to tell that city man who walks
his yappy-dog past our mailbox,
sweet corn and watermelon once grew sugary
along this bottomland, soybeans too,
cultivated by an eight-toed man
who owned but one pair of shoes.

Blink of an Eye

We said *touched*, thinking God himself
had stretched out a divine hand
to ruffle Sammy's sun-streaked noggin,
cradle his freckled face.

So proud he'd just lost his two front teeth,
folks couldn't help but pet him,
listen closely for clues to his private
word-hoard, a succinct series of whistles,
clicks, full-edged giggles, hugs
or hand-blown kisses for the lucky.

He had a knack, could eyeball tiniest
details from a distance, would point, squeal,
run a mad dash to explore.
Today it was waking to snow, icicles,
a mirror of ice stretching the pond.

His mama stirring oatmeal, be-bopping
to Bonnie Raitt, glanced out the kitchen window
too late, watched our blanket-clad boy
skid across the pond, grind to a halt,
throw up his arms, disappear.

While Light Remains

I follow backroads through neighboring
townships in the rain, graveled tracks
with names nearly forgotten,
Banjo Hill, Bean Hollow, an onslaught
of disrupted pebbles, popcorn kernels clinking
the rear wheel wells.

No doubt my Granny would advise
me to hunker down, brace for hail or worse.
I set aside my p's and q's, blast the radio,
sing along. Wipers slip-slap the beat
like two metal spoons against a thigh.
Momentarily a fool, I mourn my youth.

Fog pockets pervade the holler,
the mist an aromatherapy of triumphs
and losses, time a series of perfumed twists.
Hickories, unfazed, shimmer orange-gold
leaves like prayer flags, the sky
a baste of melted butter.

Three

Time falls like leaves, into deeper color,
joy clutches tightly to pain.

She Would Have Crawled Through Hell
on Her Belly Over Glass

Which is why I cannot tend the garden
without a tingle of nostalgia
or bear the honeysuckle's unction,
those tender tendrils. I swear

she exuded hints of that nectar
even during winter's wearisome months,
so connected was she to the land
and its ways, her eyes brimmed
in echoes of foothills and sky.

I would come to her broken.
She would cackle like a banty hen,
slap a thigh, dance a *weebly-whirl*.
Every care I thought to claim
became nameless.

When the past presses in, I kneel
as she taught me, her trowel in hand,
attend the 'taters and peas, the strawberries
plump, beginning to blush.

There's a mare in the barn, hungry for apples,
the bluebirds' box tidy and new-nested,
tree frogs *eep* and *bleedle* along the creek,
the glow of her presence so vivid,
I have to squint my eyes.

Nighthawk

Last night I dreamed my father,
twenty years gone, tried to message
me by way of bird song and frantic
flutters, pecking the plate glass window
in that Edward Hopper painting—
some primal bird beak code,
an SOS from the other side.

I am hunched over the counter,
pen and paper, marginal light,
pale as a day in February,
jotting down random letters flickering
inside my head like heartbeats,
tart against my tongue, songish
as a toddler's nursery rhyme.

My sister, out of nowhere, screams
write faster in that voice she used
when we were kids. I hand her a map
and a list of local therapists.

I feed every dogged vowel and boneless
consonant to the mouth of night,
a litany to hold off morning. But blue
dawn creeps in anyway, words piled
to the ceiling, a hundred apologies deep.

Hard Truth

Lakeside, crickets and stars,
my host says it's a Loon,
but the southeastern Ohio in me
hears coyote, the long slow wail
that comes from generations of hard luck,
skin sagging loose from the rib.

Considered the white trash of the four-footed,
you probably don't know tax dollars paid
fifty bucks a head to kill sixty-eight thousand
coyotes in 2019, or that forty-six percent
of Appalachian school-aged children
were food insecure the same year.

Tonight, moon full, air brusque,
the forsaken dream of full bellies.
Loon flaps iridescent wings,
rears her dagger-like bill,
howls Coyote's death song.

Geaux Jeaux

for Joe Burrow

Until you've fed your kids Kraft
Mac'N Cheese from the markdown bin
at the Dollar Store for the sixth time
in two weeks, made with water
instead of milk, worried sick
about what's happening to their insides;
a dented can of carrots,
past the expiration date, a luxury.

Until you've worked two jobs and still
can't climb above the food stamp line,
never mind proper heating or running water.
and you've put your six-year-old to bed hungry,
again, wondering if there is any way you can
take on a third job and still see your kids.

Until your daughter asks to pack her lunch
because she's made fun of for being subsidized,
so in desperation you take time off work
to stand in the food pantry line, in the cold,
children in tow, only to be informed
it was a tough week for the pantry, too.

Until you've put your children on the school bus,
dressed in mended clothes from the *New-2-You*,
sized for children meant to be more filled out,
and they're labeled white trash
and no amount of scrubbing can remove
that stain, and dreams of college remain just that.

Until a boy from your neighborhood
picks up a football and throws it
so far thousands of people notice,

and thousands more will eat
high on the hog, because the proof
of a person lies in their honor
and glory rests not in the moment,
but extends itself in supplication.

Vegan Mother Love

I pick up a spatula,
crack an egg—
you are there, standing
beside me on a chair,
in front of that old gas cook stove,
scrambling eggs in the skillet,
spindly legged and freckled,
minus your front baby teeth.

You know I don't eat eggs anymore,
but your stepfather does.
He walks by, chuckles, pats my bottom,
thinks my tears this morning,
are for dead baby chicks.

Grandson

Gran-mawl—long *L* for love, for laughter
and listen, even on sad mornings.
First grade, worst grade, too many
ha, ha, ha, he can't talk right.
Tender witty wisp of a half pint pug,
shedding front teeth like a waggly
spotted pup, sweat streaked hair
under a Batman ball cap.
Weekends bring cake bakes, milkshakes,
spritz from the hose, words option-*al.*

On Remembering

How mercilessly earth changes tempo.
All that was left, a gas guzzler
skidding the ice, whipped sideways,
so early it was late, you headbanged
by grievous contradiction—

the churchyard, the machine's
spasmodic scraping at glaciered ground,
the ceremony, the heartless hymn
sung by the wind, stinging our stunned faces.

No one wanted that fickle March
Monday. The daffodils, freshly bloomed,
drooped their trumpets, caught unawares,
bent and spent, their timid timbre taken by storm.

When the sun rose days later,
I faced that orb, fist raised,
thought of your body, so poorly
passed down, the subject of a headstone
and a vagary of weather.

Henhouse Anomaly

I managed to zip through three
of five errands, on a quick
trip into town, before the lack
of personal space wigged me out.

Just home, searching
for who-can-remember-what,
I hear Mr. Rogers, my Langshan rooster,
crow—a garbled cackle-lack.

I find him alone in the back yard,
tail feathers gone, marching a jagged line.

Sprinting like a pint-sized pullet,
I find all but one of the hens
inside their shack, balanced high
upon the rafters, cluckering obscenities.

Heart attack pending, I call
for my favorite, Gretta Guinea,
who darts from the woods,
flipping me her sideways stink-eye.

How quiet everyone is now.
Even the geese have hunkered down,
same name vexing every tongue,
Flucker Fox.

When the DJ Plays Bad Company During Girls Night Out After Who Can Remember How Many Tequila Shots

Please tell me I did not squeal
at the sound of those first ear-popping
guitar licks, throw my hands in the air,
kick off my pearly pink pumps,
hike up my leggings, prance
across the dance floor, shouting lyrics,
slinging the pumps round and around
a slight bend in my high-minded pointer finger.

Say I did not sweep glassware
from the table in a leap-stumble-swoop,
lemon wedges flying pith over rind,
giggle like a toddler on too much sugar,
mount the tabletop, a cock-eyed gymnast,
proceed to twist and stomp
like a goat farmer mucking out the barn,
a twist of citrus rind twining my two front teeth.

Could we keep things righteous,
grandiloquent in style, a "10" for effort,
call it badassery, not delirium—
a spirit-sloshed brain imagining
its defenseless body to be all jig and ja-ja,
versus the vigorous inventory of tortures
that await those poor old bones
come morning's first dagger of surly sunrise?

Every Song a Sigh

My family faced each Thanksgiving
with something like hope, a residual
reenactment we clung to. All of it
handily snookered by my sister's demons.

There was turkey—all the smells
you smell at your table were served
at ours, sweet corn, candied yams,
buttery biscuits, accusations.

We'd bow our heads for the blessing,
Daddy reminding us we were built to love.
Mama would shout *amen*, my sister would snort,
make fun of Jesus. Mama cried.

Outside the sky stretched
and yawned, I imagined
myself a songbird, dips and swirls,
a clear rippled coolness of breeze.

Ever since Cousin Kay got the cancer

she props herself most nights,
coughs and spits,
wages her war against
malfunctioning conduits,
questions what it is to live
as if already dead—
swallows their potions,
counts her beads,
rattles the bones,

curses the pin-wheeled
zinnias, their reds and golds
popping out of a mason jar
like misguided jesters
and the stench of loosely
turned soil that clings
to red skin potatoes tucked
alongside fresh picked
string beans and tuna casserole,
left hit-and-run on the doorstep
by cowards.

Memories are not lost
on a morning such as this—
familiar barks, sun spiking
sharp against the barn.
Kay at the window, eyebrow-less,
paisley scarfed, the hum
of children's voices and bursts
of heirloom lilac billow
her kitchen curtains, their rick-racked
hemlines snap and clack,
like a wild roll of the dice.

Packing Up at the Veterans Home

Better days, Uncle Fergus would call,
leave a message. No words, just music,
Cash or Coltrane, wicked sense of humor.
He loved him some churlish women.

I found his house shoe in the closet,
rummaged for the other without thinking.
We want to remember our loved ones
as they were when in control of their lives.

Three surgeries, each leaving less leg,
there I was, ransacking the place
for that other slipper.

Cause and Effect

After months of bereavement
and rare sightings of sunlight,
today I sat outside in a full-on burst
of it, grateful for the birds,
their flicker and tweet at the feeder.

It is hard to understand, much less
explain, the descent that comes
with loss, how needy it is,
the hundred ways it breaks you,
the spot in the chest that flares.

Just as a sparrow, rattled out
of its nest of stick-strewn meditation,
balances a branch, holds on
to a symphony longer than expected,
or a dandelion releases seed

to the wind, enshrined in strands
of pure flight, I scattered you,
handfuls of ash in the air,
every particle a scamper,
each ascension a trick of the light.

The more we ponder Aunt Mert's dementia

it is not unlike opening an attic door,
memories packed and stacked, bound by odd
bits of string, cobweb and scraps of tinsel.
Today that old white wicker headboard,
a yard-sale treasure, her first born conceived
beneath its loops and vines. An ironing board,
covered in calico, liberated, *you bet your ass,*
at the onset of polyester. That old Westinghouse
"Big Twin" window fan, whose oscillations
to her recollection, gave no ease, only recycled
that *God awful* Ohio humidity. Which one
of her kids had begged for that lava lamp?

In the corner, her trusty wooden ladder, paint-dripped,
periwinkle her favorite, used as a newlywed
for kitchen walls, knowing her mother-in-law
would throw a shit fit. The smell of sweaty boy socks,
a rusted red kick scooter and tired Barbie, whose
wee waist and taut tits cannot save her now.
Her youngest's hot pink prom dress, hand-stitched
layers of chiffon and netting, tiny sequins
sewn one-by-one, late nights, after cows
were milked, chickens put away.
Meanwhile, her split oak egg basket is worn
clean through, and *Jesus Christopher Christ,*
those sweet Brahma hens run wild, room to room,
one a dancing logroller, atop a worn basketball.

Where in the Sam hell is that green plaid suitcase
she'd threatened to use, the third time she miscarried,
and he had taken to drink the day she said,
Albert, I don't want any more babies.
And there she goes, hanging from the rafters again.
Somewhere a fluorescent light is dying,
suspension a terrible trick of the mind.

Wash Your Hands, Child

My grandmother having lived
through the Spanish flu herself,
had one rule, about which she was obsessive—
wash up, spit-polish, immediately
upon entering the house.
We could talk with our mouths full,
shove and taunt, build booby traps on the porch,
run amok in the pastures, but before
we set foot inside the house, our shoes were off,
our hands and faces scrubbed,
standing on a step stool in the washroom,
the handpump drawing water fresh from the well.

There was a bar of lye soap,
a soft wire brush and a full inspection
previous to every meal,
a *you-know-better-than-that*
whap on the backside for any slackers.

She meticulously cleaned—
every egg, pork chop, celery stalk,
jar and can before prying lose their lids,
bleach-scoured counter tops
and porcelain, floors, the bottoms
of our shoes each night.
She always laid a freshly laundered cloth
across the table before dishing up "vittles,"
most of which she had grown, preserved herself.

We gossiped about how our granny was a little off,
constantly complained as we stood in line
for that bristled brush, our bellies
grumbling nearly as loud as our mouths.

Upon her death, we let go of grandma's ways,
barely taking time to rinse our hands,
our tangibles, stuffing ourselves on-the-go,
processed foods served upsized and sugared,
licking our mucky fingers between bites.

Time is fickle and the cog turns the same
in both directions, swift-sprung.
We all tramped a slippery slope
through uncertain light, practiced
excessive predilections.
One image I can't shake:
my granddaughter, all seven years of her,
masked, standing exactly six heel-to-toe paces
away outside my screen door,
asking me how her hands, unblemished,
perfectly formed, could do me harm—
hands that had barely touched this world,
both of us spent, shaky, desperate
to blink the red out of our swollen eyes.

The Veil Between Skin and What's Inside

Days leading up to her suicide,
she said might be COVID, said better
keep my distance, said her fridge
was stocked, said fine, just fine,
said she dreamed us young
riding rockets made of tin and wire,
said tired, so very tired,
said the air smelled like an old man's
sleep-breath, said the crows
would give her no peace,
said *Rubber Soul* was the best album
ever wrought, said God, she loved
thunderstorms, rain puckering the soil,
said she wished she'd painted
her toenails, memorized bird calls,
said her cell phone was about to die,
said my voice was an echo
of our mother's broom...

Because You Were Always So Eccentric

Crows came—swear to God,
pecked at windows, nosey as
church ladies in sleek bleak choir robes,
squawked perilous predictions.

But even they, fleet feathered,
urgent, Goth as teenagers
at a Bauhaus concert,
could not best destiny.

Here you are ash and bone
and perfectly pulverized pelvis,
urn bronzed and banal, etched
in shifting shapes and small Buddha.

The funeral fiduciaries
perch side by side, their slaty,
buzzard-backs hunched,
rasping the lurid details.

How could you know
the pelvis, dense and rigid,
does not degrade inside the roaster,
must be man-handled, coaxed,
pounded into powder?

Like Dickinson on Death

Shaking off vapors of sleep, I step outside
to the promise of spring's lanky light,
blink, rub my eyes. Fog syphons the mist,
dense threads dull the landscape,

dampen my skin. I am thrown off,
transported—a sodden Sabbath in the holler,
a reunion of souls, generations gathered
to lay our saintly grandmother to rest.

Alongside the wails and gnashing
on that gray-grained dawn,
a sudden sparkle of dew, so brilliant
it stunned us to silence, opened us,
as if to warm our grievous wound.

Past worldly woes, emptiness
and suffering, our bottled-up lives
unleashed, we clung to one another,
like morning glory blossoms to a fencerow,
so brief our time in the sun.

Reincarnation

If asked, I would choose
a bush bean, stringless,
I want to stay tender and green,

camouflaged for days inside
leafy lime plumules, umbilicaled
to others likewise inclined,

not taking any shit from
the city cousins, half-runners,
all with commitment issues.

When my time comes,
I will puff my pod, wriggle to the front,
chant, *pick me, pick me,*

knowing the boil up that awaits—
the dance, the heat,
the bubble and fizz.

ACKNOWLEDGMENTS

The author gratefully acknowledges the following publications in which poems in this collection first appeared, sometimes in slightly different versions.

Appalachian Places: "She Would Have Crawled Through Hell on Her Belly Over Glass"

CALYX: "State Route 32 Appalachian Highway"

Change Seven: "Granny Medicine"

Clover, A Literary Rag: "Photo 1985"

Cutleaf: "Bada Bing Bada Boom," "Bet You Think You're Special," "Me Oh, My Oh," "Mostly a Cage Is Air,"

Green Mountains Review: "Because My Ancestors," "On Remembering," "When Nature Takes Back One of Her Own"

Gyroscope Review: "It Isn't Ever Delicate to Live"

Infection House: "Wash Your Hands, Child"

MacQueen's Quinterly: "Bad Company," "That Plus Fifty Cents"

New Ohio Review: "Mysterious Ways," "Our Grandmother"

ONE ART: "Amesville Girls," "Hanky-Panky Poker," "Hard Truth," "How Could a Woman," "True Grit," "Where We Come from Can Break Us"

Pine Mountain Sand & Gravel: "Legitimate Cockamamie"

Pirene's Fountain: "Like Dickinson on Death," "The Dogwoods at Night," "While Light Remains"

Red Earth Review: "Ever Since Cousin Kay Got the Cancer," "Sweet Corn and Watermelon"

Rock & Sling: "No Word from Kandahar"

Salvation South: "Golden Hour"

San Pedro River Review: "Fool's Spring"

Sheila-Na-Gig Online: "Because You Were Always So Eccentric," "Blink of An Eye"

Still, The Journal: "After the Farm, the Apartment on Hope Drive," "Serving"

Stirring: "Cause and Effect," "Eye of Newt, Toe of Frog"

SWWIM: "Land Lessons"

2River View: "The Veil Between Skin and What's Inside"

"Family Curse," "Henhouse Anomaly," "I Can Explain," "Nighthawk," and "Pawpaws Are Ripe" were published in *Anthology of Appalachian Writers*, Volumes XII and XV, ed. Sylvia Bailey Shurbutt (Sheridan Books, 2021 and 2023).

"Reincarnation" was published in *The Power of the Feminine "I" Anthology*, eds. Donna Biffar and Christal Ann Rice Cooper (Thresh Press, 2023).

"Geaux Jeaux" was published in *The Athens News* and also on the Joe Burrow's Heisman Speech [Facebook] Fundraiser for Athens County Food Pantry, where it went viral and was seen by over 101,000 people, resulting in thousands of dollars donated to the pantry.

"Serving" and "The Thing About Your Dad" appeared in *Serving*, a chapbook (Crisis Chronicles Press, 2018/2020).

"Spring in the Hollow" was published by the mAppAthens Poetry Trail Project (2018), produced by Ohio University Outdoor Museum Project, Athens, Ohio, and was reprinted by the Ohio Arts Beacon of Light Project (2020), sponsored by the Ohio Arts Council.

A very special thank you to Jennifer Stewart Miller for her soft touch and extraordinary care.

ABOUT THE AUTHOR

Kari Gunter-Seymour

 is the Poet Laureate of Ohio. Her poetry collections include *Alone in the House of My Heart* (Ohio University Swallow Press, 2022) and *A Place So Deep Inside America It Can't Be Seen* (Sheila-Na-Gig Editions, 2020), winner of the 2020 Ohio Poet of the Year Award. A ninth-generation Appalachian, she is the editor of *I Thought I Heard A Cardinal Sing: Ohio's Appalachian Voices,* funded by the Academy of American Poets and the Andrew W. Mellon Foundation, and the Women of Appalachia Project's anthology series *Women Speak.* Gunter-Seymour is a retired instructor in the E.W. Scripps School of Journalism at Ohio University; an artist in residence for "Writing the Land," and a Pillars of Prosperity Fellow for the Foundation for Appalachian Ohio. Her work has been featured at *About Place Journal, New Ohio Review, Rattle, Verse Daily, World Literature Today, The New York Times,* and *Poem-a-Day.*

The Places That Hold
John Davis Jr.
Davis' fifth collection of poetry praises the dusty morning light of citrus farming and the pleasures of fatherhood as it explores the darkness of places like the infamous Dozier Reform School in Florida's panhandle. Intertwining past and present with rural life, social justice, and the value of family, *The Places That Hold* offers readers a glimpse into the lesser-known corridors of the Sunshine State.

Exquisite by September
Shayla Hawkins
How is an American Black woman to navigate and maintain her sanity in a nation fraught with racism, pestilence, misogyny, and political upheaval? By turns humorous, melancholy, and sensual, this collection is a poetic museum through which Hawkins, as curator and guide, shares glimpses into different facets of her being.

Outside the Frame
Catherine Pritchard Childress
Seeking to subvert tradition in the pursuit of truth, these poems move seamlessly between worlds—the biblical and the contemporary, the mythical and the uncomfortably real. The speakers here reflect not the poet, but any woman, all women, from Lot's wife to housewife—unnamed, unheard, yet unrelenting. Set in ancient history or contemporary Appalachia, these poems rage and sing, disrupt and reconcile.

Intimacies in Borrowed Light
Darius Stewart
Stewart's first book-length collection of poems coalesces around themes of love, addiction, violence, sexual identity, and the corporeal body to betray the intimate moments that illuminate, especially, Black gay male experiences.

What We Take With Us
Sylvia Woods
Ranging from the humble and poignant to the humorous, Woods' poems explore her personal experience as an educator, as well as her own transition from daughter to mother and eventually to grandmother. Throughout Woods' work, the memory of family and the myth of family history is a driving force.

www.ingramcontent.com/pod-product-compliance
Lightning Source LLC
Chambersburg PA
CBHW031246120626
46545CB00007B/2674